CONTENTS

kids draw

CATS, KITTENS, LIONS & TIGERS

CHRISTOPHER HART

WATSON-GUPTILL PUBLICATIONS

For Francesca

Senior Editor: Candace Raney
Editors: Alisa Palazzo and Julie Mazur
Designers: Bob Fillie, Graphiti Graphics, Inc. and Sivan Earnest
Production Manager: Hector Campbell

First published in 2001 by
Watson-Guptill Publications,
a division of BPI Communications, Inc.,
770 Broadway, New York, N.Y. 100303
www.watsonguptill.com

Based on *How to Draw Cats, Kittens, Lions & Tigers*,
first published in 1999 by Watson-Guptill Publications

Library of Congress Catalog Card Number: 00-111773

Printed in Singapore

First printing, 2001

1 2 3 4 5 6 7 8 / 08 07 06 05 04 03 02 01

INTRODUCTION

Are you a cat lover? Do you love cute cats, fluffy cats, spoiled rotten and nasty cats? Then grab this book before another cat lover snatches it from you!

This book will teach you how to draw all sorts of cats, from the pampered pedigrees of Park Avenue to the lovable strays of back alleys. You'll also learn to draw proud lions, cute lion cubs, and ferocious tigers.

Believe it or not, cats' bodies are a lot like people's bodies. That may sound crazy, but this book will show you how it's true. And once you "get" how cats' bodies work, it will be much easier for you to draw them. You'll see, once you know the secrets!

You'll also learn some important principles of drawing—ones that even professional cartoonists use. You'll learn how to use overlapping shapes, how to make your characters look round and solid, and how to draw them from different angles. You'll even learn how to dress your cartoon cats in crazy costumes!

Most of the cats in this book are simple to draw. I've also included a few harder ones because I believe that, with practice, you'll be able to draw these, too. So, partner, what are you waiting for? Grab a pencil and some paper and let's get started!

CAT BASICS

 et's begin with the basic head. Then we'll move on to expressions, body types, and paws.

Drawing the Head

Here is a cute cat that's easy to draw. You'll use the same basic steps later to draw more advanced cats.

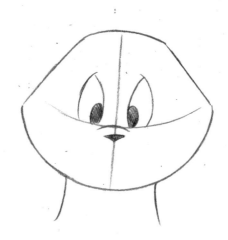

Start with a basic head shape. Draw two lines for guidelines. Put the eyes on the horizontal line. Put the bridge of the nose in the center.

The mouth is three semicircles: two for the upper lip and one for the chin. Add smile lines, eyebrows, and ears.

Add a line inside each ear and shade in the lower half. For the whiskers, use fast pencil strokes.

Add some typical markings, and you're done!

It's important to learn to draw cats from any angle so you don't get stuck drawing only one or two poses. Here's a typical cartoon cat head shown from different angles.

PROFILES—LEFT AND RIGHT
The most common mistake people make is not realizing how much mass there is to the back of the head. Cats have very short snouts (noses).

3/4 VIEWS—LEFT AND RIGHT

The law of *perspective* says that things closer to you will seem larger than things farther away. From the 3/4 view, the near side of the face should be bigger than the far side. So, the near eye, eyebrow, ear, and cheek, should be drawn slightly larger.

THE PLANES OF THE FACE

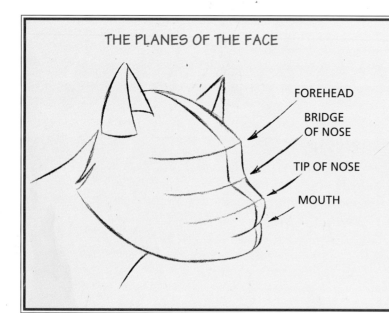

FOREHEAD

BRIDGE OF NOSE

TIP OF NOSE

MOUTH

SOUND

EAR TURNS TO HEAR

DRAWING THE EAR

Think of the ear as a cone with one side lopped off. Cats' ears usually face forward. When a cat is listening to something behind itself, its ear turns back. Cats' ears also turn back (and flatten out) when they are afraid.

3/4 VIEW—REAR

Unusual Angles

Once you become comfortable drawing cats' heads, you'll be able to draw them from any angle.

HIGH ANGLE
A *high* angle means that you are up high, looking *down* at a character. You see a lot more of the forehead.

LOW ANGLE
A *low* angle means that you are down low, looking *up* at a character. You see the bottom of the jaw.

Head Shapes

You can draw cats with
many kinds of heads.
But they all come from
the same basic cat shape.

Modeling Cats after People

To draw a cat with personality, try using a person as a model. You know lots of different types of people. Just pick one, then draw your cat with a similar expression.

FRIENDLY

CONFUSED

ANGRY

Cats That Stand Like People

Your cat can stand on four legs or on two legs, like a person.
If your cat stands on two legs, use a pear shape for its body.

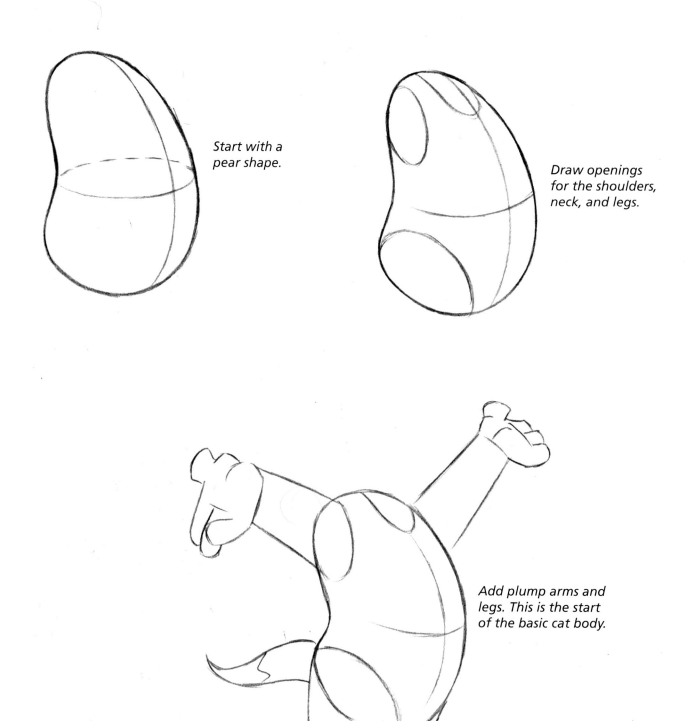

Start with a pear shape.

Draw openings for the shoulders, neck, and legs.

Add plump arms and legs. This is the start of the basic cat body.

Drawing a Standing Cat

Let's start with a basic standing pose.

Start with the shapes of the head and torso.

Draw guidelines for the head and body. Add the bridge of the nose, the triangular nose, and the ears.

Add the eyes, eyebrows, and mouth. Draw plump arms and legs.

Now for the fun stuff! Add the fingers, toes, markings on the belly, a tail, a tuft of hair, and the inner ears.

Erase your guidelines. Add long whiskers, and you're there!

More Standing Cats

Here are some more cat bodies to try.

3/4 VIEW

SIDE VIEW

SIDE VIEW (BODY) WITH FRONT VIEW (HEAD)

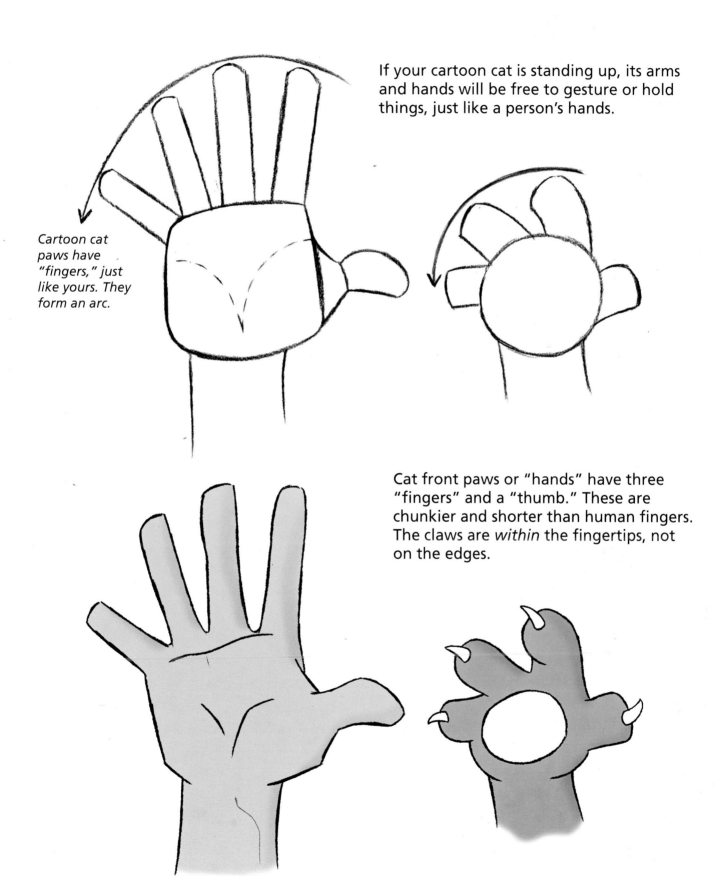

If your cartoon cat is standing up, its arms and hands will be free to gesture or hold things, just like a person's hands.

Cartoon cat paws have "fingers," just like yours. They form an arc.

Cat front paws or "hands" have three "fingers" and a "thumb." These are chunkier and shorter than human fingers. The claws are *within* the fingertips, not on the edges.

Popular "Hand" Poses

Think of the cat's "hands" as mittens. The fingers are bunched together and the thumb is separate.

MAKING A POINT

EXPLAINING

STYLISH GESTURE

CLAWING (FRONT AND BACK)

POINTING

PAW
When a cat isn't doing anything, its "hand" goes back to being a paw.

GRIPPING

STYLISH POINTING

AT REST

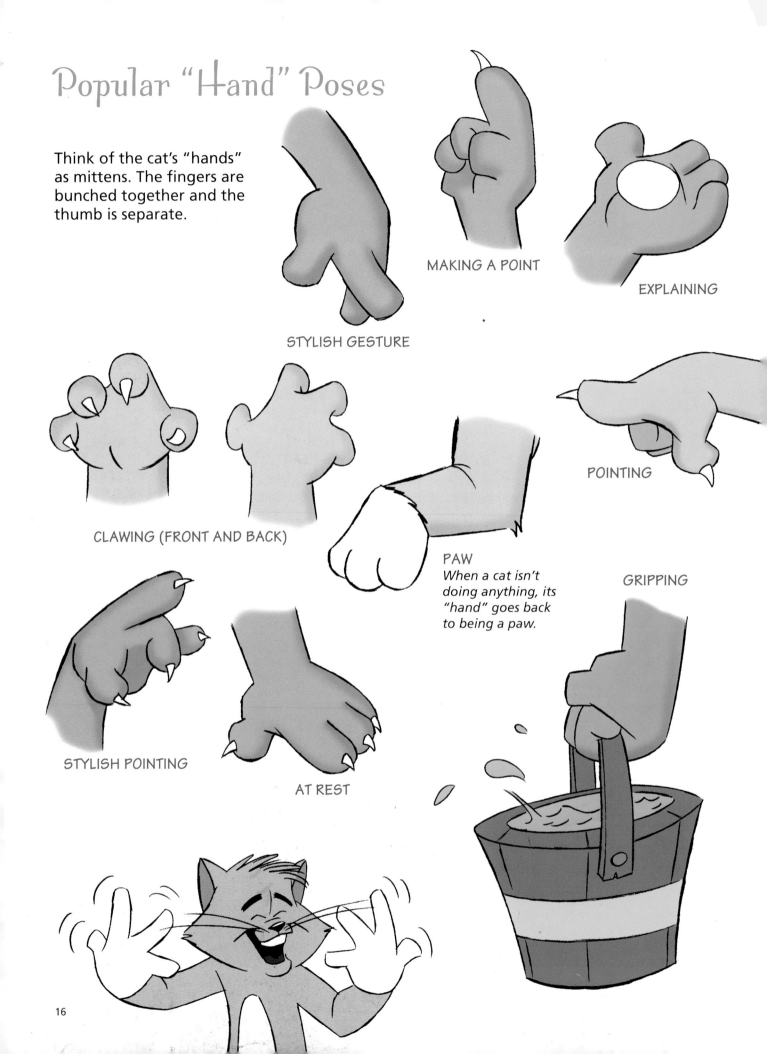

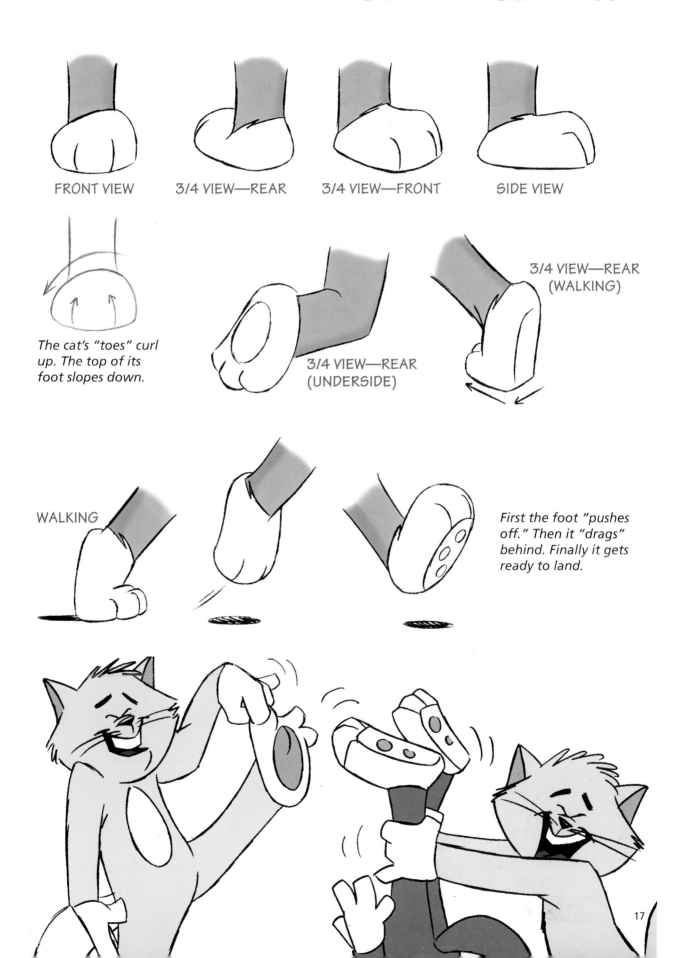

FRONT VIEW 3/4 VIEW—REAR 3/4 VIEW—FRONT SIDE VIEW

The cat's "toes" curl up. The top of its foot slopes down.

3/4 VIEW—REAR (UNDERSIDE)

3/4 VIEW—REAR (WALKING)

WALKING

First the foot "pushes off." Then it "drags" behind. Finally it gets ready to land.

Cats That Stand on All Fours

You can also draw a cat standing on all four legs.

Start with two overlapping circles for the body. This will help the body look solid and real.

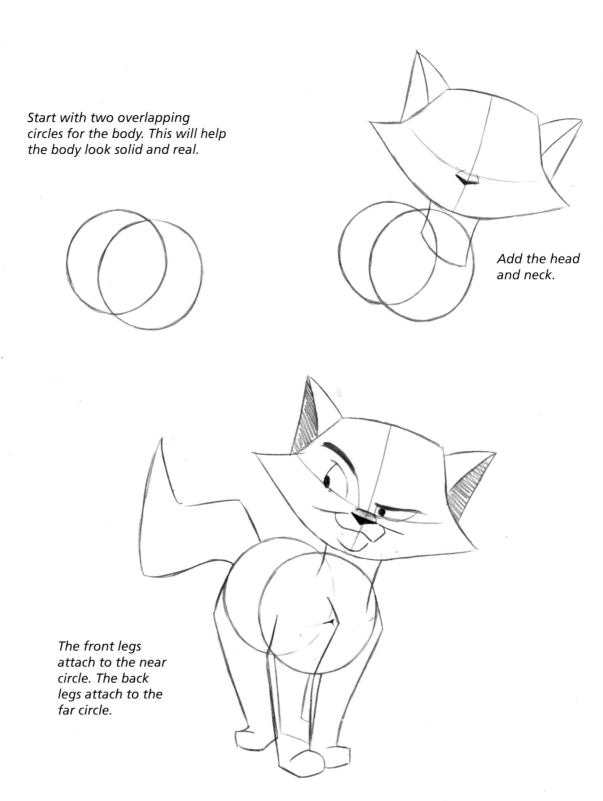

Add the head and neck.

The front legs attach to the near circle. The back legs attach to the far circle.

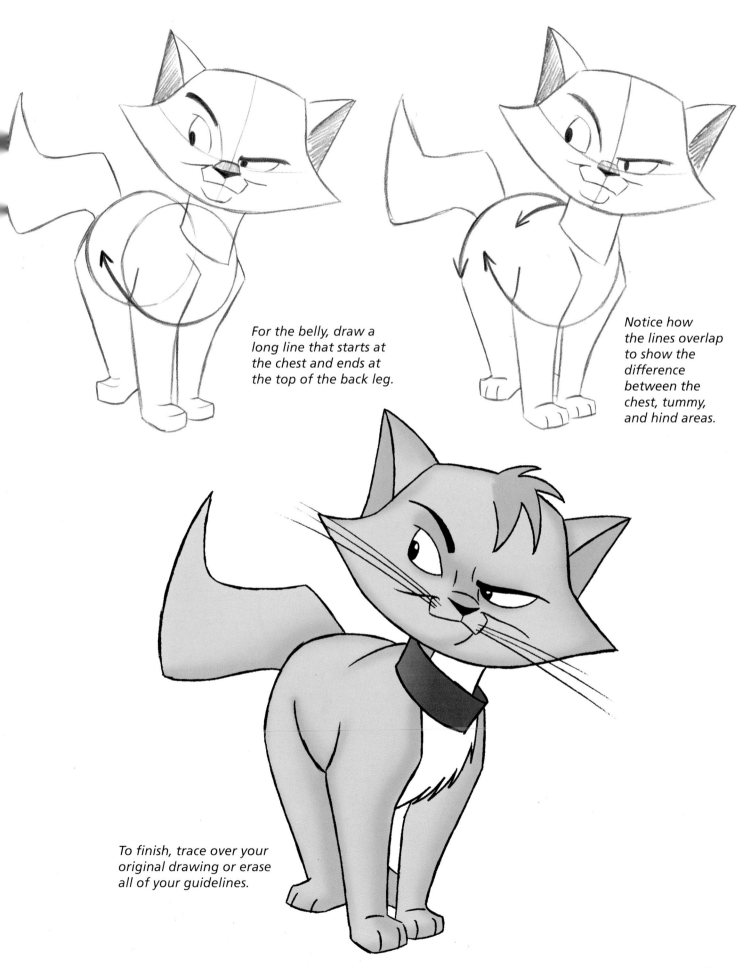

For the belly, draw a long line that starts at the chest and ends at the top of the back leg.

Notice how the lines overlap to show the difference between the chest, tummy, and hind areas.

To finish, trace over your original drawing or erase all of your guidelines.

More Cats on All Fours

Using overlapping circles makes it easy to draw cats in many different positions.

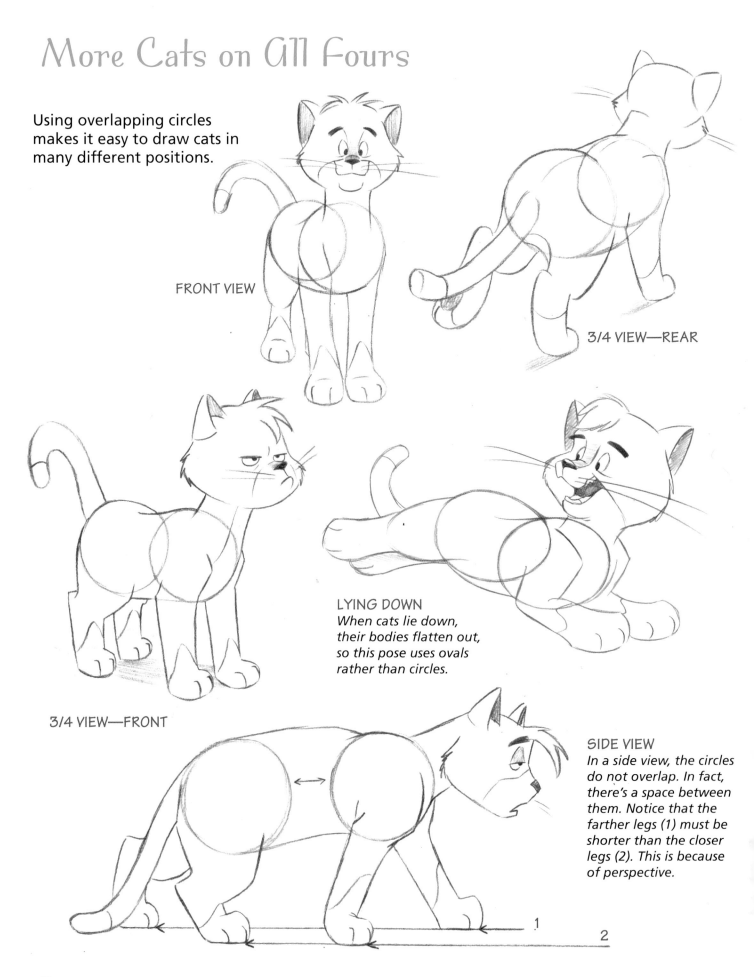

FRONT VIEW

3/4 VIEW—REAR

3/4 VIEW—FRONT

LYING DOWN
When cats lie down, their bodies flatten out, so this pose uses ovals rather than circles.

SIDE VIEW
In a side view, the circles do not overlap. In fact, there's a space between them. Notice that the farther legs (1) must be shorter than the closer legs (2). This is because of perspective.

1

2

Here's an easy trick. Draw the front and back legs on the same side of the body first. Then draw the legs on the other side. This makes it easier to space them correctly.

Draw the marking on the belly with one long, sweeping line.

HOW CAT BODIES WORK

Both cats and people have elbows, knees, heels, and toes—they're just arranged differently. Once you understand that, it will be easy to understand how a cat's body works.

SHOULDER

ELBOW

KNEE

HEEL

TOES

WRIST

FINGERS

CAT FORELEG VS. HUMAN FOREARM

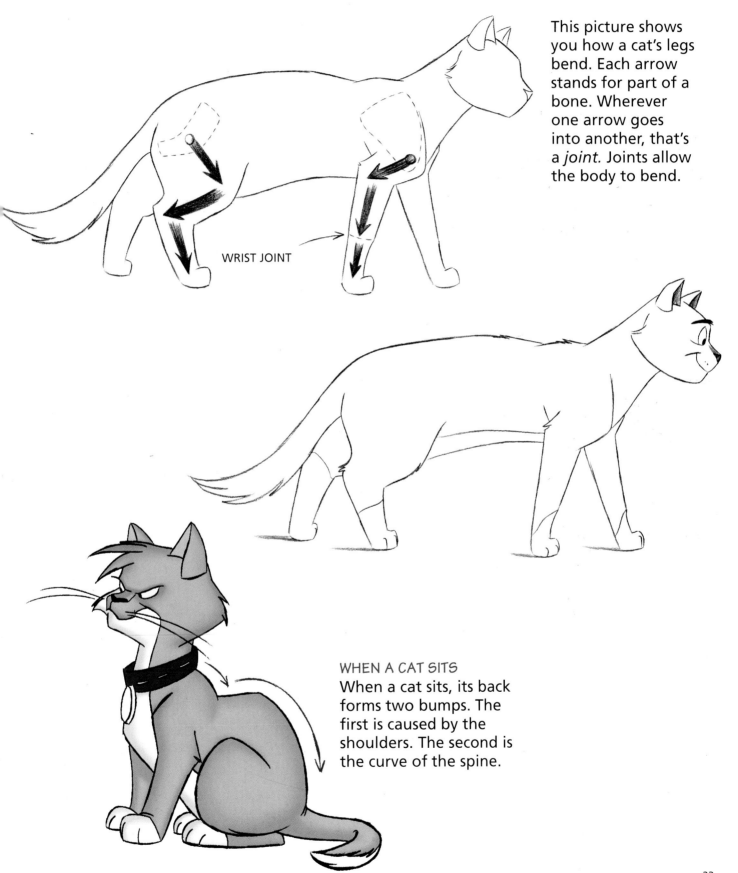

This picture shows you how a cat's legs bend. Each arrow stands for part of a bone. Wherever one arrow goes into another, that's a *joint*. Joints allow the body to bend.

WRIST JOINT

WHEN A CAT SITS
When a cat sits, its back forms two bumps. The first is caused by the shoulders. The second is the curve of the spine.

23

Cat Stretches

Cats love to stretch. They put their whole bodies into it!

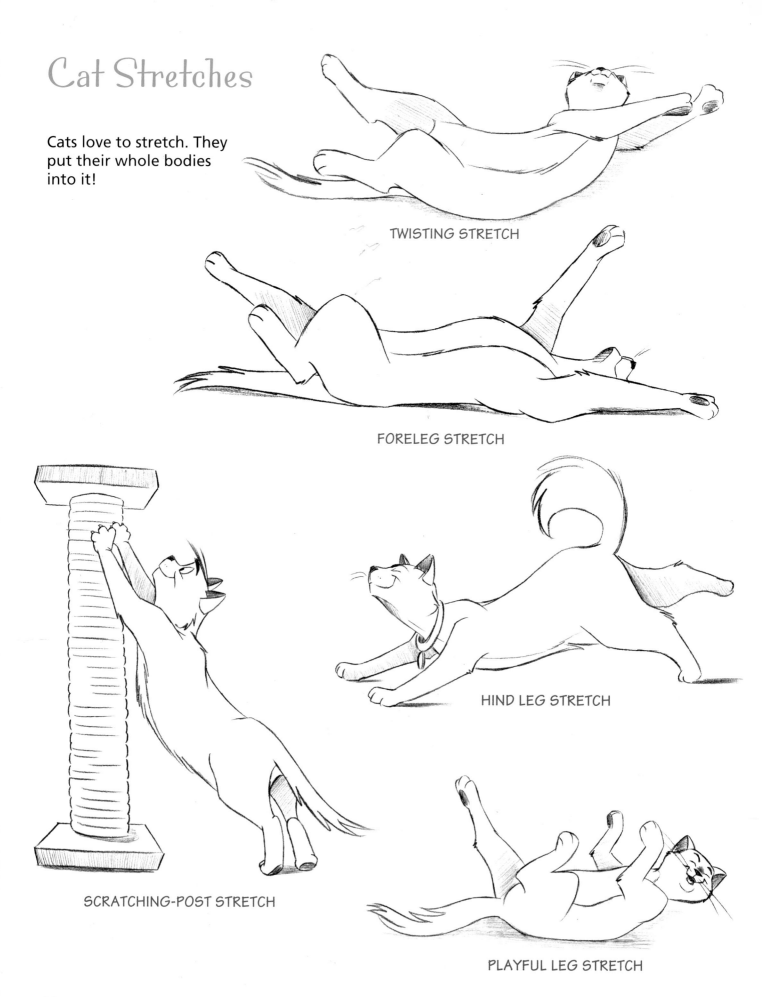

TWISTING STRETCH

FORELEG STRETCH

SCRATCHING-POST STRETCH

HIND LEG STRETCH

PLAYFUL LEG STRETCH

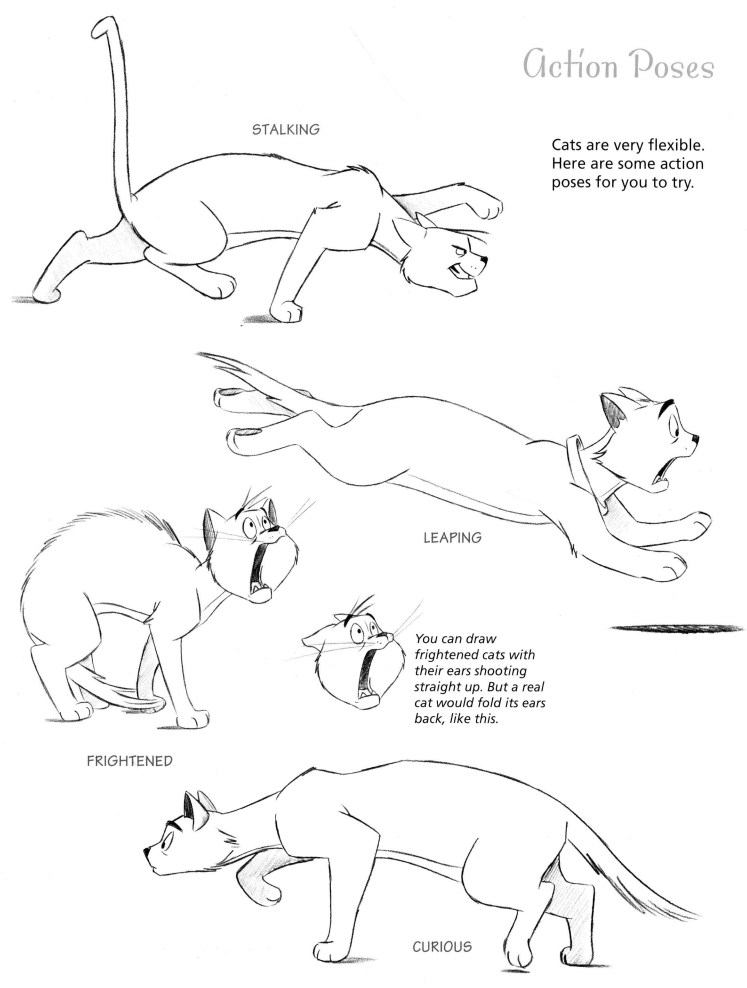

STALKING

Cats are very flexible. Here are some action poses for you to try.

LEAPING

You can draw frightened cats with their ears shooting straight up. But a real cat would fold its ears back, like this.

FRIGHTENED

CURIOUS

CAT CHARACTERS AND COSTUMES

Now let's have some fun drawing all sorts of feisty, lovable, mischievous cats.

The Stray

The stray is the "mutt" of the cat world—always looking for a handout. Add a few marks here and there to make him look shaggy. (He hasn't been groomed in a while!) And give him bright eyes. After all, this boy lives by his wits!

Crabby Cat

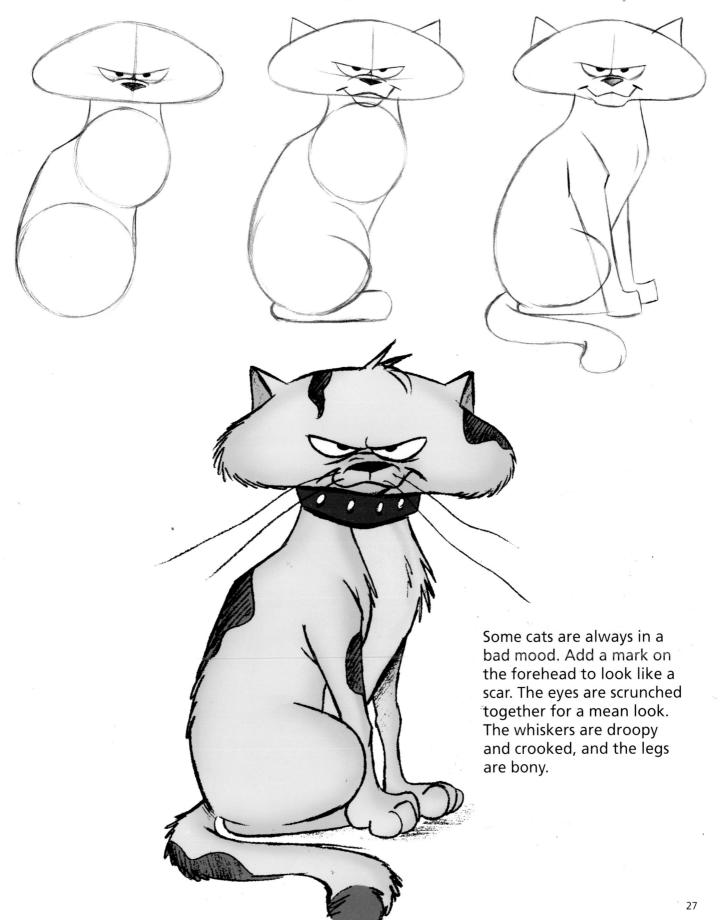

Some cats are always in a bad mood. Add a mark on the forehead to look like a scar. The eyes are scrunched together for a mean look. The whiskers are droopy and crooked, and the legs are bony.

Fat Cats

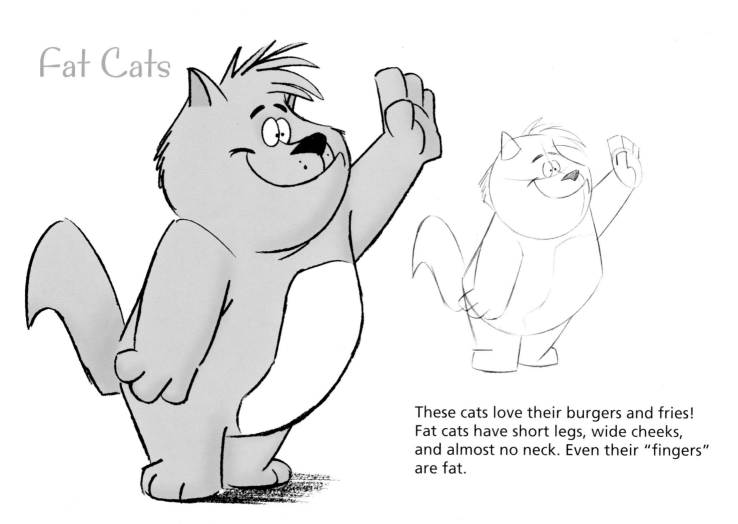

These cats love their burgers and fries! Fat cats have short legs, wide cheeks, and almost no neck. Even their "fingers" are fat.

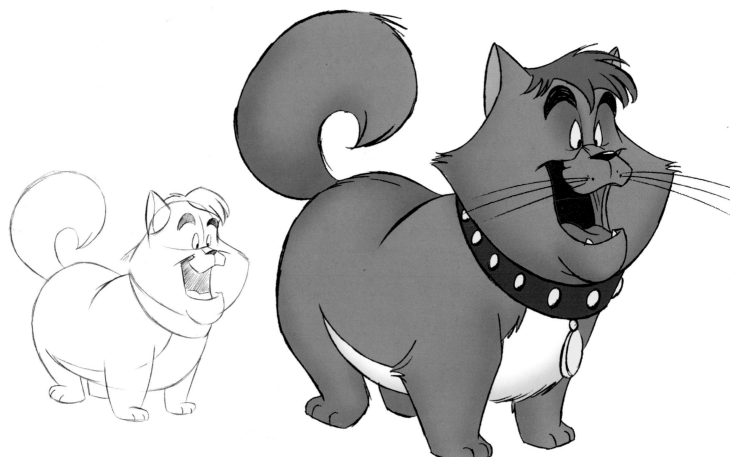

Nervous cats should look as though they are frozen with fear. Everything is stiff—hair, whiskers, and tail. Add sweat, raised eyebrows, and surprise lines around the face.

Fluffy Feline

This one's a hair ball factory.
Keep her plump and give her
a ruffle of fur here and there.

Meeeooooow!

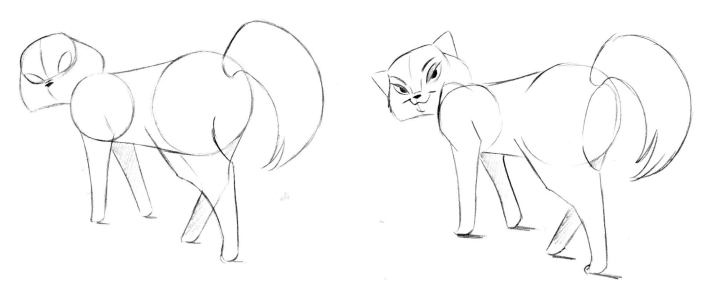

This cat's body is soft and fluffy. Her tail is bushy. Her legs taper to small, delicate paws. She has long hair and a tiny nose. Her eyes are big and dreamy, peeking out from heavy eyelids.

Cat Slob

This fat cat has definitely taken eating a step too far! Notice how putting small hands and feet on a big body makes the body look extra large.

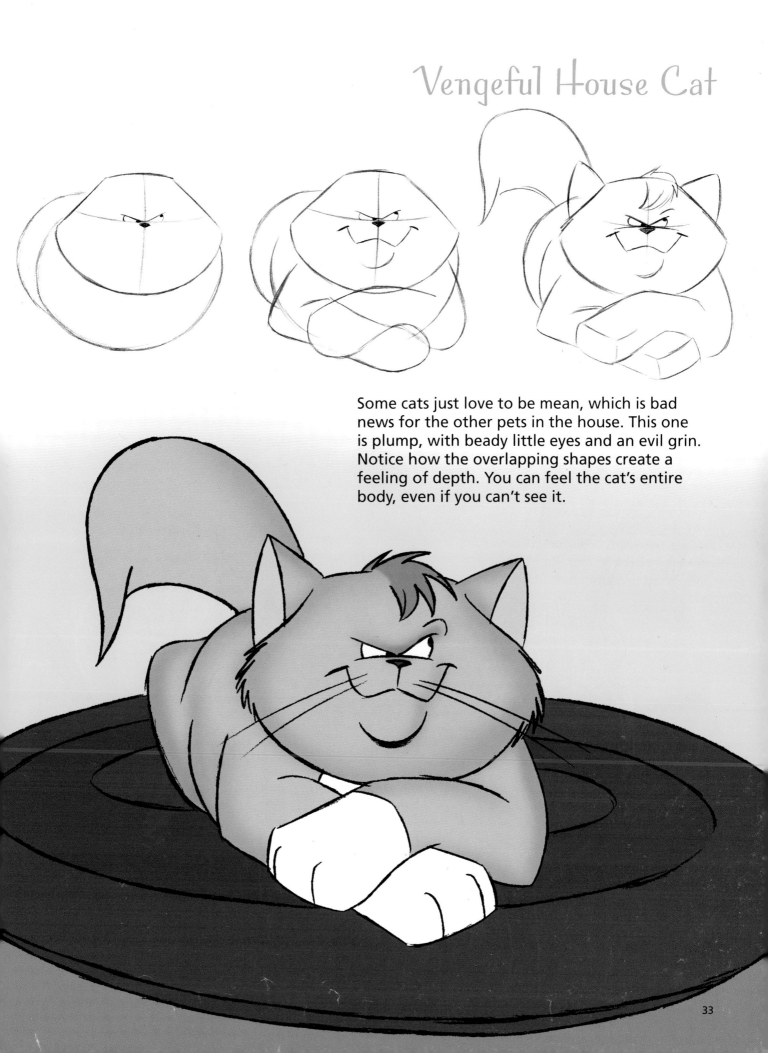

Some cats just love to be mean, which is bad news for the other pets in the house. This one is plump, with beady little eyes and an evil grin. Notice how the overlapping shapes create a feeling of depth. You can feel the cat's entire body, even if you can't see it.

Stylized Cats

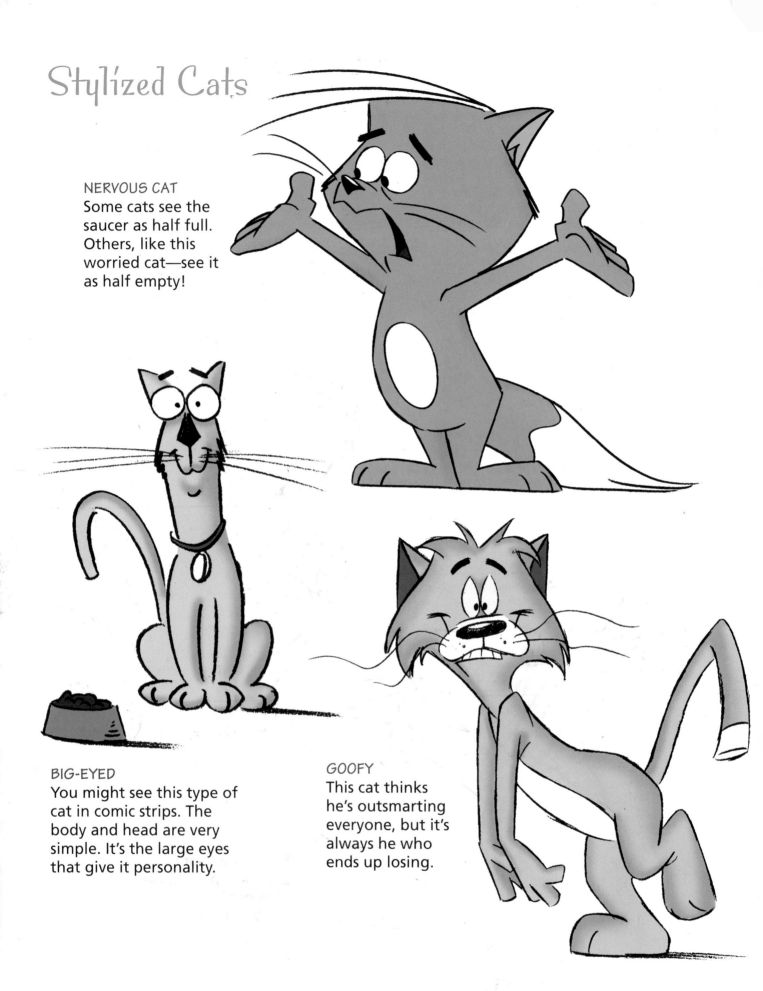

NERVOUS CAT
Some cats see the saucer as half full. Others, like this worried cat—see it as half empty!

BIG-EYED
You might see this type of cat in comic strips. The body and head are very simple. It's the large eyes that give it personality.

GOOFY
This cat thinks he's outsmarting everyone, but it's always he who ends up losing.

EDGY
To make your cat look edgy, just give him big oval eyeballs with pupils "floating" in the center.

SHORT STUFF
Short stuff has a big nose and little chin. He's also on the scruffy side.

JOLLY
If you give your cartoon cat a plump body, his arms and legs should also be plump.

Costumed Cats

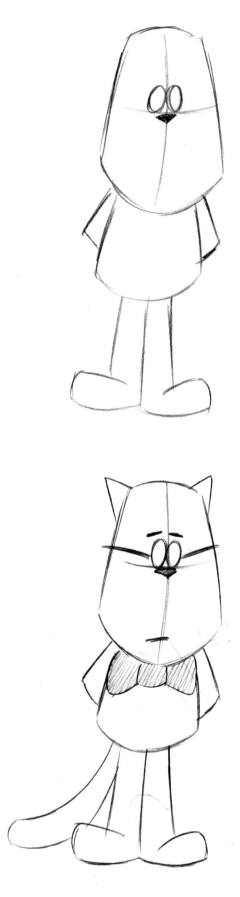

A few pieces of clothing are all you need to give your cat extra personality.

THE INTELLECTUAL
To draw a smart cat, try adding glasses. He should also have a large forehead. (It's crammed with important thoughts!) Give him a small mouth, short body, and long, skinny legs. This guy spends more time reading than he does chasing mice!

THE BLIND DATE
A jacket and a bow tie let us know this cat's dressed up. He doesn't need pants, shoes, or a hat.

Outrageous Costumes

This space cat sports the latest in 22nd-century intergalactic clothes: helmet, gloves, boots, belt, and space suit.

Funny Scenes

Putting your cats in funny surroundings is another way to show their personalities.

UNDER THE WEATHER
Cartoon animals can be more than just pets. Your cat can have a job, live in its own house, and have a family, just like a person.

HUNTING FOR "LEFTOVERS"
Alley cats are always looking through
trash cans for old food. Delicious!

AH, THAT LOOK OF LOVE

Spring is in the air, and she's got her eyes on this poor little fella. Notice the hearts over her head. They help tell the story. And notice his surprise lines, which give him a little "shudder."

KITTENS

A kitten's head is much larger, compared to its body, than the head of an adult cat. Other things are also different. Its ears and eyes are oversized, while its nose is tiny and its mouth is small. This helps it look cute.

Drawing the Head

Drawing a kitten's head is as easy as drawing a bunch of simple shapes.

Start with the basic head shape. Draw the guidelines.

The bridge of the nose goes where the two lines meet. Add the eyes and a small circle for the mouth area.

Add lines from the bridge of the nose to the eyebrows. Draw triangle-shaped ears and a thin neck.

The mouth is made of three shapes: two for the upper "lip" and one for the chin.

Add lines around the cheeks to show where the fur will be.

Draw smile lines. Shade in the inner ears. Add the furry cheeks and a tuft of hair.

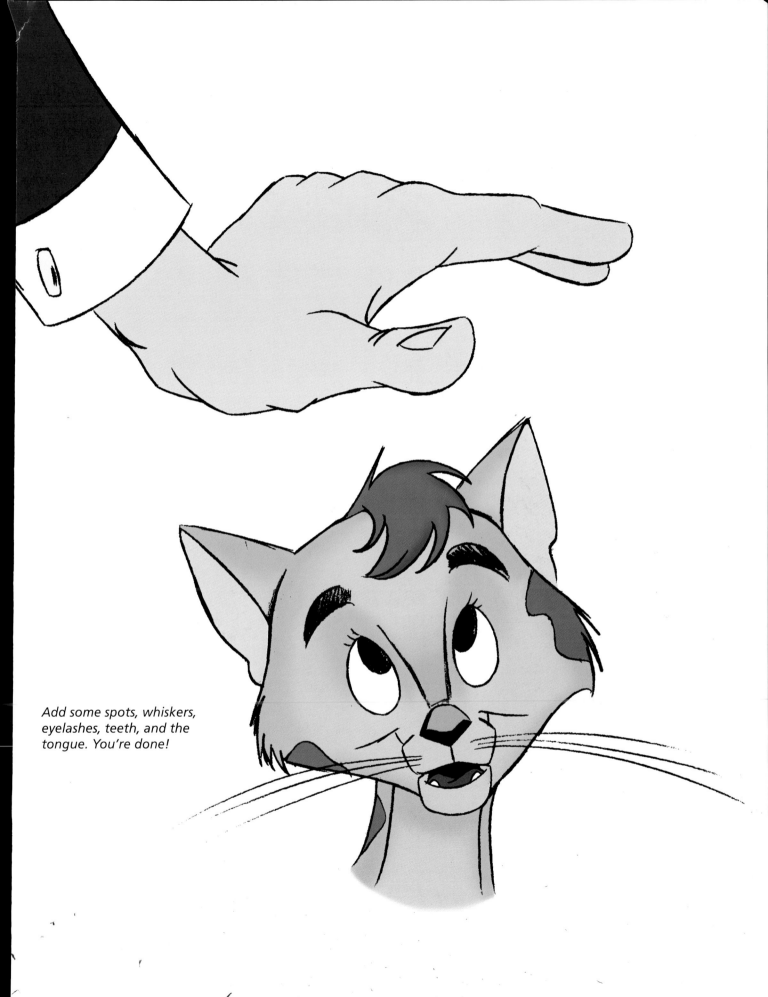

Add some spots, whiskers, eyelashes, teeth, and the tongue. You're done!

Sitting Kitty

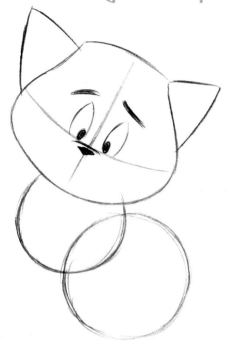
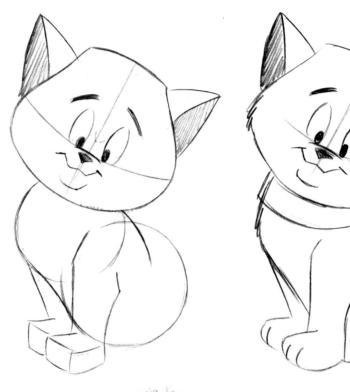

Kittens are always pudgy. They have thick legs, oversized paws, and short tails. Since a kitten's forehead is high and its eyes are spaced far apart, the middle of the forehead is a great place for a spot or marking. If you add a collar, make it look too big.

Your drawings should have a path of action that leads the eye in a circle.

PLAYFUL KITTENS
Kittens are frisky. They love to play, often with just a sock or a tennis ball.

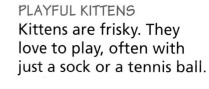

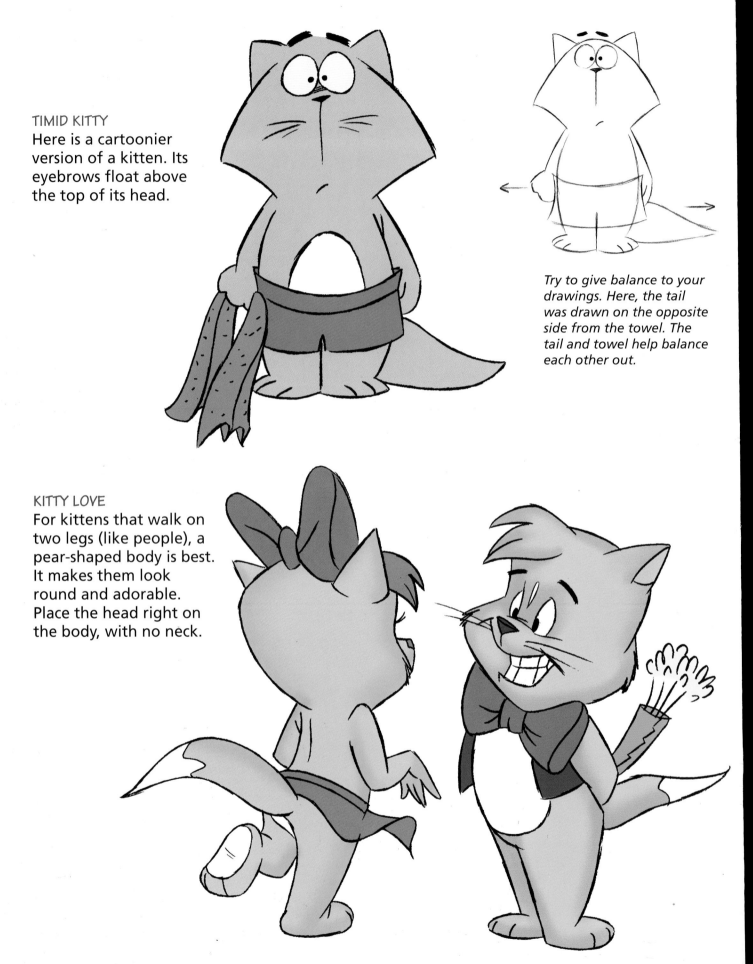

TIMID KITTY
Here is a cartoonier version of a kitten. Its eyebrows float above the top of its head.

Try to give balance to your drawings. Here, the tail was drawn on the opposite side from the towel. The tail and towel help balance each other out.

KITTY LOVE
For kittens that walk on two legs (like people), a pear-shaped body is best. It makes them look round and adorable. Place the head right on the body, with no neck.

"THE DOG ATE MY HOMEWORK!"
Yeah, right. When drawing a scene about kittens, draw it from the kitten's point of view. Here, the upper half of the teacher is cut off. This is how a little kitten would see things.

KITTENS VS. CATS
A kitten's head takes up much more of its body than a cat's head does.

LIONS AND TIGERS

Lions and tigers are powerful beasts. But they don't always need to look scary—they can also be silly, goofy, shy, or anything else you can imagine.

Draw the basic head shape.

Add guidelines. Put the horizontal one very high on the head. Draw the eyes and the nose.

Drawing the Lion's Head

For this front view, use *foreshortening* to show the lion's long nose. Foreshortening is a way of showing how shapes come toward you in space. Just make the bridge of the nose larger toward the bottom (as it comes toward you) than at the top near the eyes.

Make a mark for the mouth. Add the mane. Notice that the mane creeps over onto the forehead, just like the hair on people.

Erase your guidelines. You're done!

The Lion Profile

When drawing the profile, remember that the lion has a very long face.

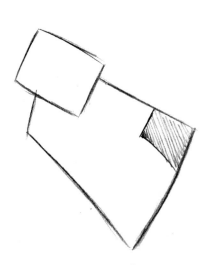 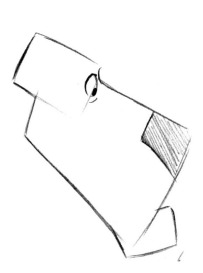 

Make the top of the head small and the bottom very big.

Add the bottom jaw and the eye.

Erase most of the guidelines. Add an ear and an eyebrow.

Add a huge mane.

49

Lion Bodies

The lion has a massive neck, chest, and shoulders. Give your lion a slim waist and make its legs thick and muscular.

3/4 VIEW

The line of the chest flows into the line of the stomach.

SIDE VIEW

Notice the slope of the hips.

ADVANCED 3/4 VIEW
This view may take a little more practice to tackle, but it's worth it.

Funny Lions

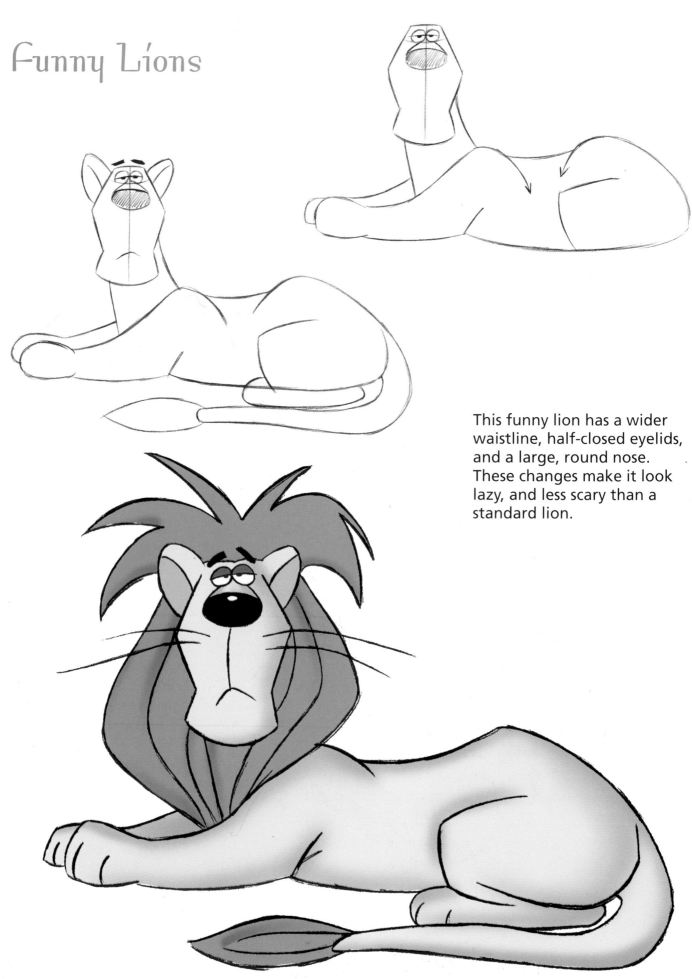

This funny lion has a wider waistline, half-closed eyelids, and a large, round nose. These changes make it look lazy, and less scary than a standard lion.

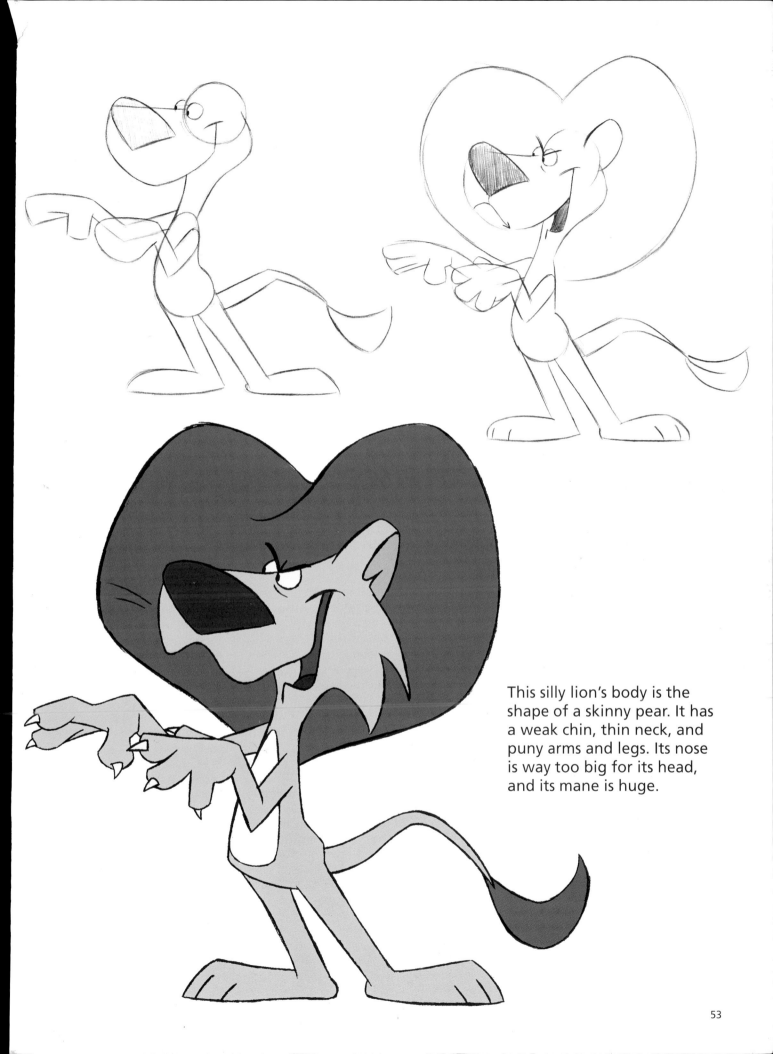

This silly lion's body is the shape of a skinny pear. It has a weak chin, thin neck, and puny arms and legs. Its nose is way too big for its head, and its mane is huge.

Plump Lion

This lion is very easy to draw. Its legs are just straight tubes.

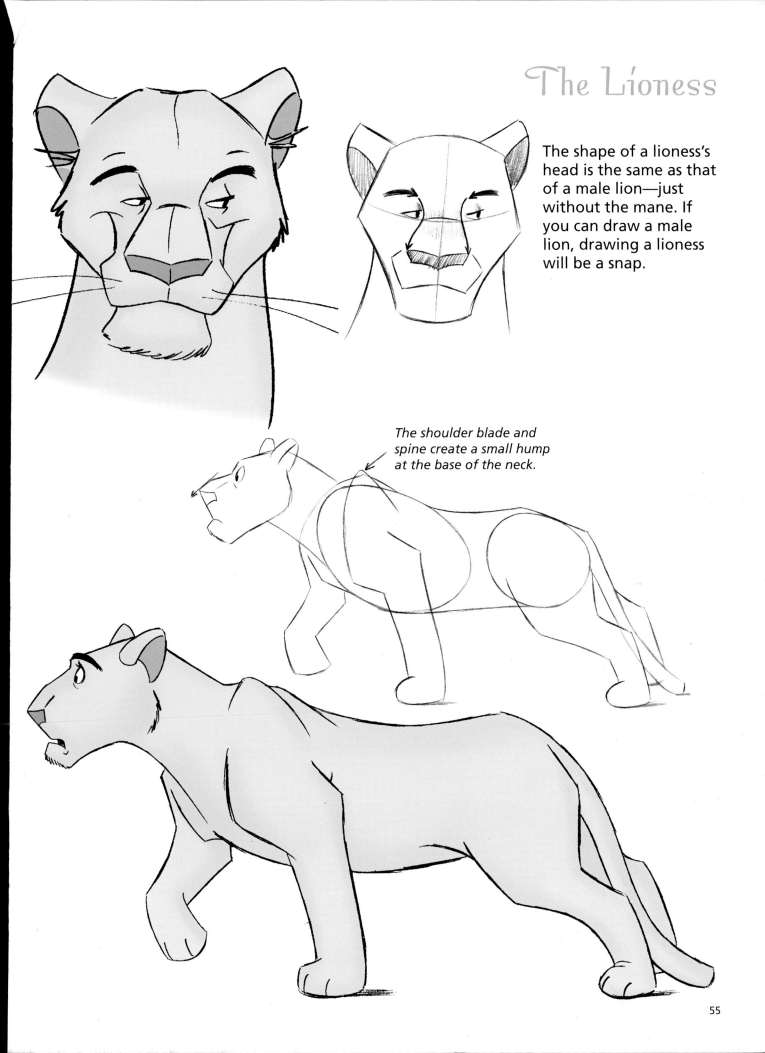

The Lioness

The shape of a lioness's head is the same as that of a male lion—just without the mane. If you can draw a male lion, drawing a lioness will be a snap.

The shoulder blade and spine create a small hump at the base of the neck.

Lion Cubs

Trees are favorite resting places for lions and cubs. With their sharp claws they can climb high up for great views (or snoozes!). This also keeps them out of danger. Give your lion cubs big paws, stocky bodies, big cheeks, small noses, short whiskers, and slightly large ears.

LION OR TIGER?

Is this a lion or a tiger? It's hard to tell without the mane or the stripes.

Here's the same character with stripes. Now you know it's a tiger.

If you take away the stripes and add a mane, it looks like a lion. So which is it: a lion or a tiger? The answer is: If you draw stripes, it's a tiger; if you draw a mane, it's a lion.

Drawing the Tiger's Head

Let's try the basic front view of a tiger's head.

Start with an upside-down half-circle. Place the eyes near the top.

The nose is like a lion's, only a little thinner. Tiger ears are pointier than lion ears.

Add stripes and whiskers, and you've got yourself a tiger!

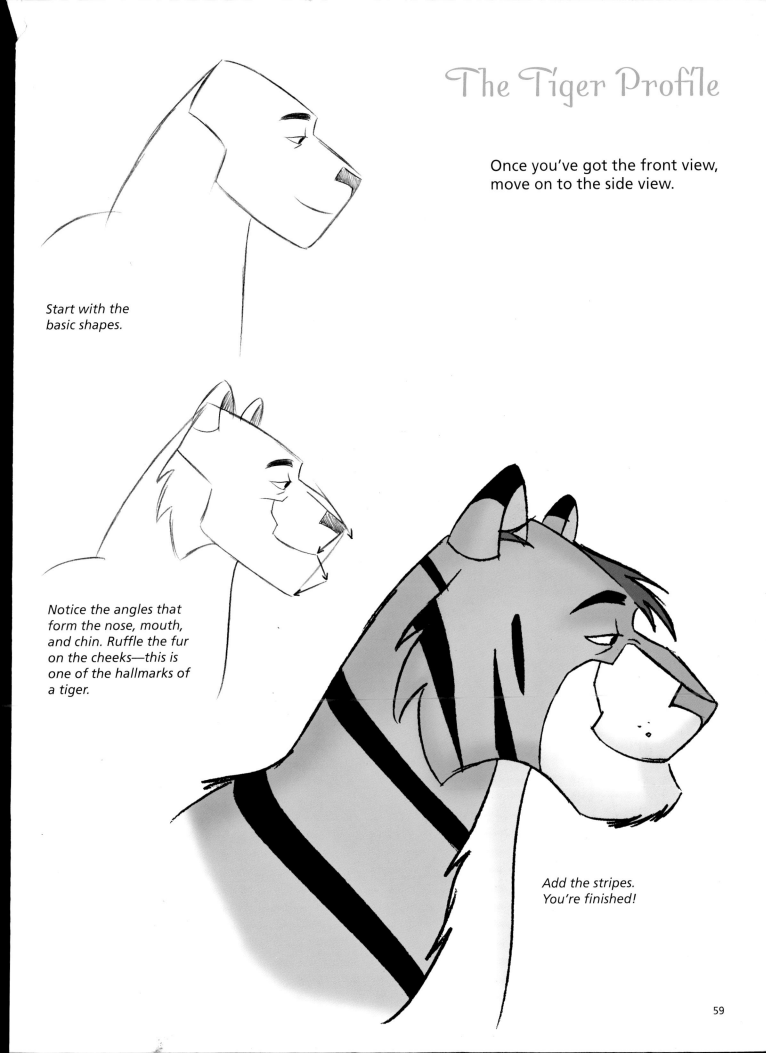

Once you've got the front view, move on to the side view.

Start with the basic shapes.

Notice the angles that form the nose, mouth, and chin. Ruffle the fur on the cheeks—this is one of the hallmarks of a tiger.

Add the stripes. You're finished!

The Classic Tiger

The tiger is one of the most beautiful creatures on earth. Did you know that tigers are slightly larger than lions?

The Tiger Body

To give this tiger a meaner look, I've made its waist really narrow. This makes the chest look larger.

Draw the basic forms.

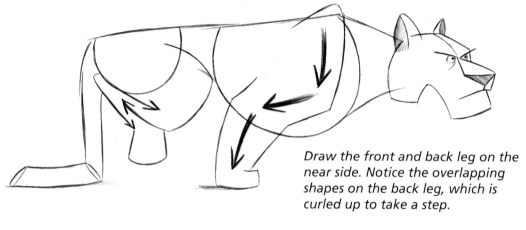

Draw the front and back leg on the near side. Notice the overlapping shapes on the back leg, which is curled up to take a step.

Add the front and back legs on the far side. Draw the tail, which hangs low.

Finish with some broad, sharp stripes.

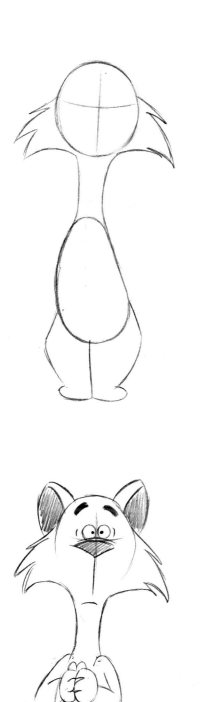

Any animal, no matter how ferocious, can be drawn to look harmless and even goofy. This silly tiger has a thin chest, long neck, and no chin. Its tail is too long for its body. If I were planning a scene with this guy, I'd have him tripping over it.

INDEX